UnCaged

HOW TO BREAK FREE FROM A TOXIC RELATIONSHIP AND REDISCOVER YOUR VOICE AND POWER

Lavonne Nichols

TO: ______________________________

FROM: ______________________________

ISBN: 978-1-0881-4102-1
Nichols, Lavonne

UnCaged: How to Break Free From a Toxic Relationship and Rediscover Your Voice and Power

© Copyright 2023 - All rights reserved.

Cover Design: Lavonne Nichols
Cover and Book Layout: Kantis Simmons, The SIMAKAN Group

All rights reserved. No part of this guide may be reproduced, transmitted, or distributed in any form or by any means without permission in writing from the publisher except in the case of brief quotations embodied in critical articles or reviews.

Legal & Disclaimer
The content and information in this book are consistent and truthful, and it has been provided for informational, educational, and business purposes only.

The content and information in this book have been compiled from reliable sources, which are accurate based on the author's knowledge, belief, expertise, and communication. The author cannot be held liable for omissions and errors.

Dedication

With love and gratitude, I dedicate this book to the pillars of my strength, my mother, Diana Nichols, and my brother Timothy Nichols. Your unwavering support and encouragement have guided me through every challenge and triumph. Your love has given me the courage to pursue my dreams, and I am forever grateful for that.

As I pen these words, I am reminded of my beloved father, John Nichols, whose love for music was the cornerstone of my passion. Though he is no longer with us, his legacy lives on in every note I play, in every melody I compose, and in every word I sing. Dad, thank you for instilling in me the power of music to heal, unite, and spread love.

To my dear family, you are the foundation upon which my dreams have taken flight. Your love and support will forever be etched in my heart and the soul of every song and book I write.

TABLE OF CONTENTS

Introduction

The room was full of people, but I felt utterly exposed. It was as if they could hear every thought in my head, every beat of my heart, and melody I was singing.

But when I spoke, really spoke, they couldn't hear a thing. It was as if my voice was lost in translation, my pain invisible to the world around me.

So I retreated to my cage, my haven, hoping that the next time I opened my mouth, someone would hear me. Someone would see through my smile and hear the cries of my heart, coming to my rescue before it was too late.

In my cage, I wrote my songs and poured out my pain onto the pages of my notebook. The tears that fell were like fuel, igniting every verse with a passion that couldn't be ignored.

My iPhone became my confidant, my voice recording app my sanctuary. It was the one place where I could speak freely, without fear of judgment or repercussion.

Sadly, I know that countless women can relate to my story. Women who have found themselves in situations they never thought possible, living lives they never imagined. I used to believe that certain things would never happen to me, but I was wrong. I was trapped, caged like a beautiful songbird with nowhere to fly and nowhere to sing freely.

The cage represented the trauma and toxic relationship that held me back, preventing me from being my true self. Once my greatest gift, my voice was lost, and I didn't know how to find it again.

People surrounded me but still alone, looking out at the world from behind the bars of my cage.

Trauma comes in many forms, from illness and injury to loss and heartbreak. It can also be severe, such as rape or torture.

In this book, we will focus on relational traumas, the types of traumas that leave lasting scars on our hearts and minds.

These are the traumas that can lead us to feel trapped, caged, and unable to find our voice. But there is hope.

Through my own journey, I discovered that healing is possible and that it begins with finding the courage to speak our truth.

I want to take an opportunity to share more about what trauma is and what types of trauma one can experience before we go deeper into my journey so there is clarity.

Acute trauma, also known as Big "T" Trauma, is the result of a single stressful or dangerous event. It can include:

- Severe illness or injury
- Violent assault
- Sexual assault
- Traumatic loss
- Mugging or robbery
- Being a victim of or witness to violence
- Witnessing a terrorist attack
- Witnessing a natural disaster
- Road accidents
- Plane accidents
- Military combat incidents

- Hospitalization
- Psychiatric hospitalization
- Childbirth
- Medical trauma
- Post-suicide attempt trauma
- Life-threatening illness or diagnosis

Little or Small "T" Trauma are everyday experiences that can be expected as a part of life.

- Loss of a loved one (not traumatic bereavement)
- Moving to a new house
- Losing a job
- Interpersonal conflict
- Infidelity
- Divorce

- Abrupt or extended relocation
- Legal trouble
- Financial worries or difficulty

Chronic trauma is the result of repeated and prolonged exposure to highly stressful events. The following are examples of chronic trauma:

- Receiving regular treatment for a long-term, serious illness
- Sexual abuse
- Domestic violence
- Bullying
- Exposure to extreme situations, such as a war, being a refugee, homelessness, etc.

Complex trauma is the result of exposure to multiple traumatic events.

- Abandonment
- Physical abuse or assault
- Sexual abuse or assault
- Emotional abuse
- Witnessing violence or death
- Coercion or betrayal. This often occurs within the child's caregiving system and interferes with healthy attachment and development.
- Sibling abuse
- Domestic, and family violence
- Emotional neglect and attachment trauma
- Verbal abuse
- Long-term misdiagnosis of a health problem
- Bullying at home, school, or in a work setting

- Physical neglect
- Overly strict upbringing, sometimes religious
- Civil unrest

(Admin, 2022)

Trauma can affect anyone, regardless of background or social status. Whether it's acute trauma from a single event, chronic trauma from prolonged exposure to stress, or complex trauma from multiple traumatic experiences, the effects can be devastating.

This book primarily focuses on romantic relationship trauma, but the resources and strategies can be applied to other types of traumatic experiences.

During my own experiences with trauma, I found myself just existing, but not truly living. I was numb; my spirit detached from my physical body. I could talk to people, but my mind was always foggy, consumed by my traumatic experiences. But I found a way through it all, and in this book, I will share my journey of healing and resilience.

I will discuss how I coped with trauma through the arts, specifically singing and songwriting. I will also share how I stayed motivated to achieve my goals, even when it felt like the weight of my trauma was too heavy to bear. Through my personal experiences and education, I will provide you with practical tools and strategies to overcome your own trauma and become more resilient. This book is not just about surviving trauma, but thriving in spite of it.

How to use this book

Welcome to the journey of healing through this book. Each chapter is designed to provide you with tools, reflection moments, quotes, and songs to support your healing journey.

Reflection Moments

In the Reflection Moments section, you'll have the opportunity to delve deeper into the key messages of each chapter and relate them to your personal experiences. The questions asked are intended to provoke introspection, encouraging you to consider how the topics covered in the chapter have shown up in your life and what can be changed to support your personal growth goals.

Reflection allows your brain to pause amidst chaos, untangle and sort through observations and experiences, consider multiple possible interpretations, and create meaning. Once you have meaning, you can learn from it and shape your future mindset and actions.

Quotes

The Quotes section features insightful sayings from various people who have shared their wisdom on the topics covered in this book. These reinforcing quotes will provide you with additional inspiration and encouragement to continue your healing journey.

Songs for Healing

The Songs for Healing section offers you the power of music to support your healing journey. Music has the ability to transport you to a place in time when you heard the song and felt joy, sorrow, inspiration, and pain. Listening to, singing along with, or creating music can reduce depression and anxiety, even in high-stress jobs. Music helps us to be resilient by reinterpreting difficult experiences to be less threatening.

You don't need to have previous musical experience to tap into the power of music for healing. The idea is not to create a Grammy award-winning song but rather to utilize your creativity to support your healing process. If you desire to take songwriting to a professional or more recreational level, check out the resources prepared for you on saysomethinggoodllc.com. For the purpose of this book, especially if you don't already have a background in music, I want you to use instrumentals (music that has no words) to create your songs. The instrumentals can be from any genre; the music just needs to inspire you to write words to go along with it. Start by thinking about your life experiences and what you want for your life moving forward, and just begin writing. Do not overthink the process. I encourage you to use songwriting as a form of journaling. You can choose to write an original song, write the words to a meaningful instrumental, or use them as writing prompts in a journal.

****Please know that if you create a song using an already produced instrumental you cannot claim rights to the entire song only the lyrics you created.*

Disclaimer:

I want to make it clear that I, Lavonne Nichols, am not a licensed mental health professional. However, I am a certified trauma-informed life coach and a survivor with years of experience committed to trauma healing, education, community facilitation, and peer work.

The resources shared by Say Something Good LLC are not intended to replace professional mental health help, but they can provide relational support and information to aid your healing journey.

Recovery from trauma is a unique experience for everyone, and seeking professional help can guide you to find the right path for you. In case of an emergency or crisis, there are resources available such as:

The Crisis Text Line (www.crisistextline.org) provides free and confidential support through online chat, text, or phone.

You can also find a helpline or hotline near you at www.findahelpline.com.

If you or someone you know is struggling with suicidal thoughts, please reach out to the National Suicide Prevention Lifeline at 800-273-8255 or text "HELLO" to the Crisis Text Line at 741741 for immediate help.

For those who need help with domestic violence, please call the toll-free number 800-799-7233 (SAFE).

Chapter 1

Accept the Situation

"Music has a way of touching our spirit that goes far beyond words just spoken."

-Lavonne Nichols

During my season of complex trauma, I was in a haze and didn't realize the gravity of the situation.

I was ashamed to admit that I had overlooked the red flags and didn't see some things right away.

However, I had to accept that I was in an extremely toxic relationship and that I needed to change what I had the power to change in the situation.

Acceptance means that you are choosing to understand the situation and move forward. It means that you are choosing peace, strength, and sanity over pain, fear, and craziness.

It doesn't mean that you are in agreement with what happened to you, but you accept that it happened, and you are allowed to feel sad and hurt.

You accept that there is more to life, and you have the power to continue writing your story.

Sometimes we are in denial and don't want to see the truth. We may hide what's really going on from ourselves and the world. However, it's vital to accept what happened so that we don't take on the victim mentality.

Should I accept the victim mentality?

Signs of the victim mentality include

- avoiding responsibility,
- placing blame elsewhere,
- making excuses,
- not seeking possible solutions, and reacting to most life hurdles with "it's not my fault."

People with a victim mentality may feel

- hopeless,
- believe they lack support,
- blame themselves,
- lack self-confidence,
- have low self-esteem, and
- struggle with depression and PTSD.

Having a victim mentality is not uncommon and comes from past trauma, betrayal, codependency, and manipulation. It's crucial to accept what happened, embrace the truth, and move forward.

Acceptance is the first step towards healing and building resilience. It's not easy, but it's necessary to let go of the pain and embrace the possibilities that life has to offer.

Reflection moment

Today I want you to think about your current situation. Are you really seeing it for what it is? Have you convinced yourself that you are strong enough to conquer this by yourself and that no one else needs to know about it?

Quotes

"Letting go doesn't mean that you don't care about someone anymore. It's just realizing that the only person you really have control over is yourself."

— Deborah Reber, Chicken Soup for the Teenage Soul

Songs for Healing

I invite you to create a song that shares how you feel after reading this chapter. Or find a song that allows you to feel empowered to accept what has happened to you and makes you feel like moving forward.

____

____

____

____

____

____

____

Chapter 2

Forgive Yourself

"Forgive yourself for your faults and your mistakes and move on."

-Les Brown

Now when I say forgive yourself, this can mean something different for everyone. But overall, we all deserve forgiveness. Whether we are the abuser or the victim. Whether we are the person who has self-sabotage our life, we all deserve grace and forgiveness.

Once I realized what had happened to me.

Once I realized the key players in the story and my role in the situation, I had to then come to a place of forgiveness.

I had to forgive myself for what I allowed, my part of the story.

From start to finish, the actions that I took, as well as the choices that I made that I had control over. I had to be honest and retrace my steps and identify those small moments where I made a conscious decision to move forward when I felt something saying stop, or no don't go. It's important to be self-reflective and notice that some of our own unhealthy character traits have intensified an already bad situation.

This is not to say that abuse, violence, and manipulation are ever acceptable under any circumstances. This is about accepting, forgiving, and moving forward. I had to be honest with myself for overlooking the red flags. And I had to be honest with myself about the things that I was naïve to. So at the end of the day, I had to forgive myself. I had to say to myself, yes, I allowed certain things. But no, I didn't deserve what happened to me. I am not what happened to me. I am so much more than that.

When you forgive yourself, you are saying that when you think about this situation moving forward, you will begin the healing process to no longer allow it to inspire bad thoughts, guilt, or shame. But when you think now about that toxic relationship and the trauma you went through you will look at it as a lesson, a learning experience that will allow you to see how strong you truly are. I realize that what I went through was horrible but I see past that now. I learned more about myself from this situation and what I can overcome. Forgiveness comes when you can look back and talk about the situation no longer punishing yourself or feeling ashamed.

I also had to forgive my abuser. Now I know that may have been hard for someone to just read. If you need to take a moment, please do so. Take a deep breath. I encourage you to allow yourself to see the power of forgiveness in this moment.

I realized that I had to forgive my abuser, not because I condoned his actions or because he wasn't responsible for causing me unbelievable hurt. I had to understand that we all hurt and-have pain. We must all own our actions and take responsibility regardless of what we have been through that may have caused us pain.

Whether he did these things consciously or unconsciously. Whether he intended to harm me or was a victim of his situation. Whatever the case may be; for me to move forward with my "life," I had to forgive. They say that forgiveness is not for the person who wronged you but it's for you. That can't be any more true. I had to realize that by not forgiving myself and him; I was holding on to the situation instead of releasing it. By not forgiving, I was allowing it to take up space in my life instead of making room for new exciting healthy events and positive people to come into my life. For me continuing to hold on to the pain endured was causing damage physically, emotionally, and spiritually, which could continue to negatively impact current and future relationships and impair my productivity in other areas. In other words, by refusing to forgive, we can harm ourselves even more. Please understand that this is easier said than done. Forgiveness can bring up great pain, and conflict, and it can be messy. However, it is a part of the process to get you to live a healed and productive life.

Reflection moment

What do you need to forgive? Who do you need to forgive? How is being unforgiving holding you back from moving forward?

Quotes

Forgive yourself and welcome love back into your life.
— Wayne Dye

Songs for Healing

I invite you to create a song that shares how you feel after reading this chapter. Or find a song about forgiveness and healing.

____

____

____

____

____

____

____

____

Chapter 3

Reclaim Your Life

"It's never too late to reclaim your life. You owe it to yourself to take back what is rightfully yours and be happy."

-Lavonne Nichols

Once I accepted the situation for what it was, I could then begin to deal with it. I had to take ownership of what was happening to me and start to understand what I had control over and what I didn't. I focused on the things that I could control, but it was a process that took me several months to figure out. With the help of this book, I hope it helps you in less time than it took me.

Realizing that I was in a horrible situation wasn't enough. I had to want to get out of it, too. This is another crucial step, and I want to ensure you don't overlook it. At times, I found myself feeling sorry for my abuser and thinking that I needed to stay in the situation to help him. If I stayed, he would be grateful and treat me better. If I stayed and been a "ride or die chick," somehow he would see that I was worthy of being respected. However, this was a twisted mindset, and I don't endorse this thinking. I'm sharing this because there might be someone out there who thinks they can change someone else. That their love will somehow heal someone, and they will start making better choices or treat you differently. The truth is, only they can change themselves. They have to want it more than you do. If you find yourself in this situation, taking care of yourself and seeking help is how you can improve the situation.

Don't get me wrong, I can pray for that individual today and hope that God has done something positive in their life. However, when you're in the depths of your situation, you have to understand what's most important. As a single woman, then, I had to focus on myself. If I had children, I would have had to prioritize their well-being and mine. I couldn't continue to feel sorry for someone causing me so much pain, and I keep denying what I needed to do in order to survive. As a believer, I believe in the power of prayer and wise counsel from trusted people.

Sometimes, when going through traumatic situations, we make excuses and say things aren't bad or we don't need help.

However, that's not true. You're reading this book because you know you need help that goes beyond yourself. It was just God and me for a good portion of my journey to wholeness. But then, God allowed people to speak into my life, encourage me, and hear my struggles. I had to be open to people knowing my truth and be okay with them knowing my life despite the shame. But I was sick and tired of my situation, so I decided to let people in and be honest with myself. I sought out self-help books, videos, and wise spiritual counsel as well as mental health professionals. I created a list of essential things to do and goals to accomplish to help me reclaim my life, stay motivated, and improve my self-esteem. Looking back, I see that all of this laid the foundation for this very book.

Take responsibility for your life and move forward!

Reflection moment

Are you being honest with yourself? Do you say to yourself you're OK? Do you tell others everything in your life is fine, knowing that you often cry yourself to sleep? Why are you ashamed of your story? If you shared your story, what do you think would happen?

Quotes

"Life is 10% what happens to us and 90% how we react to it." - Charles R. Swindoll

Songs for Healing

I invite you to create a song that shares how you feel after reading this chapter. Or find a song about reclaiming your life.

Chapter 4

Reconnect With You

"The only person you are destined to become is the person you decide to be."

-Ralph Waldo Emerson

We've come a long way, and I want you to know that your progress is admirable. It takes courage to realize that you're going through a difficult time and even more to decide to overcome it. You've identified the problem, recognized your role, and chosen to forgive yourself and the person who hurt you. You've set yourself up for success, and the best days of your life are yet to come. Now it's time to reconnect with who you are and what you want to achieve from here on out. Here are some questions to ponder: What is your purpose in life? What do you want to accomplish?

In my toxic relationship, I lost myself. I lost my voice and identity, and that happy, ambitious young woman I once was faded away. My partner used to appreciate my gifts and talents, but he despised them over time. I used to sing, act, and pursue my passions fearlessly. I had my own home and car; my family and friends were my support. But he slowly chipped away at everything I had built, convincing me I was better off without them. I lived in fear, unable to be happy or express myself without facing his anger. I even began to believe I was not talented enough and had nothing to offer the world.

When we go through traumatic experiences, we often lose ourselves. We need to remember our purpose and why we matter. To reconnect with our goal, we must go back to the beginning and recall what made us happy as children. We should remember our childhood dreams and what brought us joy. What comes easily to us that others find challenging? What advice do people often seek from us? These questions can help us identify our calling and rekindle our passion.

Some of us have always known our purpose, but we got sidetracked along the way. A toxic relationship, a health issue, or a life event derailed us. It's time to get back on track and pursue what we were meant to do. Let's live life to the fullest, embrace our passions, and fulfill our purpose.

My faith in God kept me going when I wanted to give up. It helped me when I felt like I had messed up so much that I no longer deserved another chance. However, I turned to the Scriptures and spent time with God, reminding myself that I was worthy of His love and His blessings. One Scripture that has always been my favorite but meant even more to me during difficult times is Matthew 28:20b, which says,

"Lo, I am with you always, even unto the end of the world."

This reassurance let me know that even if I was at the bottom of the barrel, feeling filthy, broken, and used, God was still there with His loving arms open, inviting me to embrace His love and accept His promises. I recalled the times when I needed to sit in the bathroom tub to cry in peace, even in the middle of the day. I felt like I couldn't sink any lower, but God gave me the strength to look for signs of hope.

I was grateful when God spoke to me, letting me know that I am beautiful, loved, and not defined by my situation. He encouraged me to use my voice and assured me I still had something to give the world. He let me know that it wasn't over for me yet.

Let me tell you, although it may sound cliché, you are here for a reason. You survived that traumatic experience because the world still needs you. You are meant to live, thrive, and contribute to the community in a way only you can. I need you to believe that your life has value and that your sickness or bank account does not define you. You must still live despite the pain of losing a loved one.

And I'm not just talking about existing - I mean genuinely living a life that you can look back on years from now and rejoice that you didn't give up because life is now so amazing. I remember the day I took my life back, and although I almost lost everything, I am happy I chose to fight for myself.

Reflection moment

As you were reading this chapter, what things came to mind? Could you remember who you used to be before you were hurt? Do you remember the dreams you had for your life?

Reconnecting with your Quotes

Emotional turmoil can be a powerful catalyst to reconnect us with our divine nature. It propels us into a journey of self-discovery and urges us to learn how to love and accept our entire being. — Debbie Ford

Songs for Healing

I invite you to create a song that shares how you feel after reading this chapter. Or find a song about reconnecting with yourself and walking in your purpose.

Chapter 5

Reconnect With Your Strength

"Some people believe holding on and hanging in there are signs of great strength. However, there are times when it takes much more strength to know when to let go and then do it."

-Ann Landers

As we continue our journey toward finding ourselves after tragedy and trauma, it's important to tap into our inner strength. You've already remembered what made you happy, your dreams and goals for your life, and now it's time to dig deep and find the strength to move forward. It may feel like you're weak and helpless, but trust me; you are much stronger than you give yourself credit for.

In my last year of high school, I experienced one of the most traumatic events before entering into the toxic three-year relationship I shared earlier. My father, my hero, fell ill, and his health began to decline, making him bitter. Despite the years of turmoil, my family endured, it didn't take away the hurt I felt when he passed away in 2000, just months before my high school graduation. Before this tragedy, I knew exactly who I was and what I wanted to do with my life. I wanted to be a singer and a teacher, using my voice to change the world and educate students while singing to my community about God's goodness and hope. However, after my father's passing, I began questioning life and everything I thought I knew. I asked myself why he had to die so soon and why God would allow it. Although my father had been sick for many years, it didn't make his passing any easier to accept. Despite all these questions and the pain I was experiencing, I had to stop and think about moving forward. I had to pull from a strength I didn't even know I had at that age. And that's what I want you to do as well.

During this time, I started to remember all the good times I shared with my father and how he wanted me to live and make him proud. I began to think about his life and his choices that affected my family and me. Through this, I understood that although I had lost my father, I had gained an opportunity to learn from his life, both his successes and his failures. If I wanted to move forward, I had to consider these lessons.

It's important to note that everyone is different, and if you feel stuck or lack motivation or strength to move forward, it's okay. I've been in that situation before and know how hard it can be. When you don't know how to be strong for yourself, I encourage you to lean on your faith and trust in God. My trust in the Lord has been an anchor when I felt like I was wavering. God has been my primary source of strength, peace, and wisdom, and I encourage you to seek Him out.

In addition to God, there are people in our lives who hold us up when we feel weak. These may be family members, friends, or even strangers who believe in us. Allow them to pour into you and build up your strength.

Reconnect with those in your support system, whether family, friends, church family, life coach, or therapist. They are there to help you on your journey. Remember you don't have to go through this journey alone. Remember that you are stronger than you give yourself credit for and you can get through anything with the right support system.

Reflection moment

What are some practical ways can you strengthen your faith to strengthen your life?

____

____

____

____

____

____

____

____

Quotes

"You have power over your mind—not outside events. Realize this, and you will find strength." —Marcus Aurelius

Songs for Healing

I invite you to create a song that shares how you feel after reading this chapter. Or find a song about reconnecting with your strength.

Chapter 6

Self Confidence & Positivity

"She remembered who she was, and the game changed."

-Lalah Delia

In this chapter, we will focus on rebuilding your self-confidence and providing you with ways to improve your self-esteem through self-love techniques. You may not have realized how your self-esteem was impacted during your traumatic ordeal, especially if it was with a romantic partner or due to illness.

You may not have realized that your perception of life and yourself has changed. You may have developed self-limiting beliefs that have prevented you from moving forward. However, please don't beat yourself up because you can turn that around. It will take work, consistency, and a small amount of faith, but you can and will make huge strides in this area of personal growth.

When preparing to leave my toxic relationship, I needed to mentally and spiritually get my mind right. During this time of reflection and honesty, I realized that I was displaying characteristics that were not truly loving myself.

So much had taken place in my life that it had begun to wear on me, but because it didn't happen overnight, I failed to understand its impact on how I viewed my overall being, my talents, and even my physical appearance.

I began asking myself questions I want you to ask yourself now.

1. **Do you think negatively about yourself often?**

2. Have you found it hard to say anything good about yourself?

I remember instances when someone would compliment me, and instead of saying "thank you," I would immediately direct their attention to a flaw or shortcoming. Does this sound familiar to you?

3. Do you allow people to walk all over you?

You may say, "I am strong, and no one walks over me." However, do you tolerate behaviors from those you know are not right in your world? You know that you are being mistreated, but you feel like you can't speak up for fear of hurting their feelings or losing them entirely.

4. Do you find yourself comparing yourself to others?

As much as I see the value of social media, it has given us a false sense of the reality of others. Comparing yourself to others can make you chase a life that doesn't exist. Many people only show you the good parts, and very few offer the negative. But we all have ups and downs. We all go through stress, bad days, disappointing outcomes, and loss. It would be unrealistic to think your life is worse than others because it is not. You are just going through a difficult situation that you will overcome.

5. Do you take care of your physical body?

At first, I didn't realize it during my toxic relationship, but I had let myself go. I was so consumed by my situation that I was eating things that were not the healthiest for me. On top of that, I was not working out, which allowed me to gain a significant amount of weight. I believe that I was severely depressed, and it was starting to show on the outside how I felt on the inside.

Take these questions along with the reflection portion of this chapter and truly dig deep. You have the opportunity right now to be honest, and begin to deal with the hard truth of the matter. If the answers to your questions leave you feeling hopeless, I must tell you that all hope is not lost. You can change all of this. You can rebuild what you think you lost and truly live your desired life.

Reflection moment

What are some strategies you can use to build and maintain a positive mindset?

Quotes

"You cannot consistently perform in a manner inconsistent with how you see yourself."

– Zig Ziglar

Songs for Healing

I invite you to create a song that shares how you feel after reading this chapter. Or find a song about self-confidence & positivity.

Chapter 7

Live With Intention

"Make a commitment to grow daily."

-John C. Maxwell

This step can be one of the most enjoyable parts of the healing process, but it also presents challenges when trying to live the life you want after a traumatic experience. You've come a long way in your journey, and it's essential to take a moment to reflect on everything you've learned about yourself. Through this process, you've discovered that you're stronger than you ever thought possible, and forgiveness is vital to moving forward and reclaiming your freedom. You've also started reconnecting with yourself and those who support you on this healing journey.

Now, it's essential to be intentional about how you proceed in life. It's possible to complete all the steps in the previous chapters and still not fully embrace life again. You could settle for a mediocre life or strive to live a life that brings you joy and fulfillment daily. Happiness and peace are options in life; choosing them is up to you. You can see yourself as a victim or a survivor and decide to see the beauty in life, even during difficult times.

When rebuilding my life, I realized I needed to "live as if my life depended on it." I wanted to live an engaging life filled with love and intentionality, and it allowed me to find positivity in each day. I never wanted to be in a place where I felt like I lacked passion, opportunities to give back to my community, or validation from others. As I began to live on purpose, I realized that validation and security come from within, and God blessed me with a supportive group of friends and family to reinforce these principles in my life.

During my darkest moments, I existed but wasn't truly living. I moved through life numb and disconnected from my spirit. My fear of being seen, heard, and loved ruled my life for three years. However, once you've hit rock bottom, your outlook on life changes. I feared leaving this life without living it to the fullest. I embraced my truth and showed up daily for life, counteracting thoughts of shame and regret with activities that made me smile and contributed to my life and the world around me. I became an active participant in my own life and story.

Let me give you some actionable items to understand better what it means to be an active participant in your life. As an extrovert, I never minded being around people or going out. However, after my toxic relationship, I felt ashamed, making it hard to be around others as I thought they knew what had happened to me. I had to become strategic to reintegrate myself into my community and social settings.

First, I made a plan aligning with my purpose and where I wanted to go. I joined a gym and took group classes, making new friends with similar interests. Surprisingly, I realized my situation did not define how people saw me. It was just an inner fear that I kept validating with shame.

Next, I took myself on dates and intentionally talked to others around me, making new connections. I searched for opportunities to try new things, celebrated life, and threw myself into new experiences during my birthday.

Here are a few other things I did that you can try:

- Love authentically and freely
- Speak positively about yourself
- Invest in yourself
- Learn something new
- Help someone else or give back
- Share your testimony
- Protect your energy

Protecting your energy is one of the most important things you can do. Your energy is the driving force that helps you conquer your goals and get through your day. It's okay to say no to things that don't serve your purpose or disturb your peace. Stay away from those who drain your energy, especially in romantic relationships. Trust your spirit, and consistently pray to God for understanding and wisdom. And although it may be hard to stay positive during hard times, how you think will change your environment and keep you in peace and joy.

Reflection moment

What can you do today to help you do what you have always wanted?

Quotes

"Over time, even the tiniest meaningful actions add up, each bringing you closer to a life truer to your dreams and free of regret."

— Jane McGonigal,

Songs for Healing

I invite you to create a song that shares how you feel after reading this chapter. Or find a song about living with intention.

___

___

___

___

___

___

___

Chapter 8
Building Resiliency

"Fall seven times, stand up eight."

-Japanese Proverb

Surviving a toxic relationship is a challenging process that requires immense courage, strength, and perseverance. It's common to feel lost, broken, and hopeless after getting out of such a relationship. However, the good news is that you can heal and rebuild your life with resilience. This chapter will discuss how to build strength after a toxic relationship.

What is Resilience?

Resilience is the ability to adapt and bounce back from adversity. It's the capacity to cope with stress, trauma, and setbacks and return to well-being. Resilience is not a fixed trait; it's a skill that can be learned and developed over time. It's essential to recover from a toxic relationship and move forward with your life (American Psychological Association, n.d.).

Here are some ways to build resilience, especially after a toxic relationship:

Seek Professional Help: Professional help is crucial for dealing with a toxic relationship's emotional, physical, and psychological effects. Therapy can help you process your feelings, identify behavior patterns, and learn healthy coping mechanisms. It's essential to find a therapist who specializes in trauma and abuse and understands the complexities of your situation.

Additionally, a life coach can provide a safe and non-judgmental space for individuals to process their emotions and experiences. They can help individuals identify their needs, set boundaries, and make decisions that align with their values and goals. A life coach can also help individuals reclaim their power and agency after experiencing trauma or a toxic relationship. They can provide tools and techniques to help individuals build self-esteem, self-worth, and self-confidence.

Practice Self-Care: Self-care is crucial for rebuilding your life after a toxic relationship. It's essential to prioritize your physical and emotional health. Engage in activities that make you feel good and boost your confidence, such as eating a healthy diet, exercising regularly, and getting enough sleep. Take time to relax and do things you enjoy, like reading, painting, or gardening.

Build a Support System: Surround yourself with people who love and support you. Contact family, friends, or support groups who understand what you've been through. It's essential to have a support system that can offer emotional support, practical help, and a safe space to share your feelings.

Set Boundaries: Setting boundaries is crucial for rebuilding your life after a toxic relationship. It's essential to recognize your needs and communicate them. Learn to say no and set limits on what you're willing to tolerate. Boundaries help you establish healthy relationships and protect yourself from further harm.

Cultivate Gratitude: Gratitude is a powerful tool for building resilience. Focus on what you have and are grateful for rather than what you've lost. Cultivate a positive mindset by practicing gratitude daily. You can keep a gratitude journal or make a list to remind yourself of the good things in your life.

Reflection moment

What are your current goals or aspirations, and how can building resiliency help you achieve them? What is one thing you can do today to build your resiliency and increase your ability to overcome obstacles in the future?

Quotes

"The greatest glory in living lies not in falling, but in rising every time we fall." - Nelson Mandela.

Songs for Healing

I invite you to create a song that shares how you feel after reading this chapter. Or find a song about building resiliency.

Chapter 9

Affirmations

"Affirmations are a way of planting seeds in the garden of your mind."

- Bob Proctor

The Purpose of Affirmations

Although the use of affirmations may seem cliché, science is behind it. One critical psychological theory regarding affirmations is the self-affirmation theory proposed by Claude Steele in 1988. According to this theory, when people's self-image is threatened, they are motivated to affirm the integrity of the self. Affirmations can help counteract negative thoughts and experiences that threaten our self-image, but they should not be relied upon solely to address the root cause of the problem.

Affirmations tap into our core values and help us reinforce our self-identity. It's important to focus on affirmations that strengthen our sense of self and align with our desired self-image. Affirmations have been shown to assist in reducing negative thoughts and dwelling on negative experiences (Wiesenfeld et al., 2001).

When we use affirmations, we are reprogramming our subconscious mind to encourage us to believe our words and take action to make them a reality. Affirmations are powerful motivators for inner change and are written in present tense and first-person form, using "I" or "I am" statements. They denounce negative thoughts and focus on positive emotions.

To make affirmations effective, using them daily, ideally in the morning, before bed, or during tense situations, is important. Affirmations can be found through search engines, social media, affirmation cards, smartphone apps, or created personally. Writing affirmations down can also be very effective, making the words more powerful and personal.

The remainder of this book is dedicated to curated affirmations to help improve your life after experiencing trauma or hard times. Use them daily for at least 21 days and repeat them out loud or to yourself with boldness and confidence. You'll also find blank pages where you can create your own "I am" or "I" statements that are meaningful to you.

30 Affirmations To Improve Your Life After Trauma

1. I accept what has happened to me without judgment or blame.

2. I am excited to start my next chapter.

3. I am love; I feel love; I see love.

4. I release all the pain I have felt, and I embrace healing.

5. I embrace the present moment with openness, curiosity, and acceptance.

6. I love myself and permit myself to be happy.

7. Setbacks are opportunities for growth and learning.

8. I am allowed to say how I feel; my feelings are relevant.

9. Attracting love starts with self-love.

10. What I am doing today is getting me closer to my goals.

11. I forgive myself for mistakes I made when I didn't know better.

12. I have overcome this situation.

13. My body is worthy of love and respect.

14. I choose to prioritize my mental health.

15. I have all the resources I need to overcome this difficulty.

16. I have friendships that are real, genuine, and loyal.

17. I am resilient and capable of overcoming challenges.

18. I am in charge of my feelings; today, I choose peace.

19. I choose calm over worry and faith over fear.

20. I am strong enough to rise above my negative thoughts.

21. I express my needs and seek help with compassion and vulnerability.

22. I am stronger than my current situations.

23. I persevere through difficulties with courage and determination.

24. I am deserving of support and assistance.

25.I am safe, and I am ok.

26.I no longer let people's opinions of me affect me.

27.I am more than my anxiety.

28.I am allowed to take time to heal.

29.I accept myself just the way I am.

30.I am living God's true purpose for me - an abundant, loving, healthy life full of joy.

Notes & Your Affirmations

Notes & Your Affirmations

Notes & Your Affirmations

Notes & Your Affirmations

Works Cited

Admin. (2022, September 02). What is trauma? Retrieved January 14, 2023, from https://www.centerforanxietydisorders.com/what-is-trauma/

American Psychological Association. (n.d.). Building Your Resilience. Retrieved from https://www.apa.org/topics/resilience/building-your-resilience

Andriote, J.-M. (no date) How music heals and inspires us in challenging times, Psychology Today. Sussex Publishers. https://www.psychologytoday.com/us/blog/stonewall-strong/202107/how-music-heals-and-inspires-us-in-challenging-times?eml

Types of trauma. (2020, December 18). Retrieved January 14, 2023, from https://traumapractice.co.uk/types-of-trauma/

"Self-Affirmation Theory ." International Encyclopedia of the Social Sciences. . Retrieved December 20, 2022, from Encyclopedia.com: https://www.encyclopedia.com/social-sciences/applied-and-social-sciences-magazines/self-affirmation-theory

Steele, C. M. (1988). The psychology of self-affirmation: Sustaining the integrity of the self. Advances in Experimental Social Psychology, 21(2), 261-302.

Raypole, C. (2019) Victim mentality: 16 signs and tips to deal with it, Healthline. Healthline Media. Available at: https://www.healthline.com/health/victim-mentality#signs

Wiesenfeld, B.M., Brockner, J., Petzall, B., Wolf, R., & Bailey J. (2001). Stress and coping among layoff survivors: A self-affirmation analysis. Anxiety, Stress and Coping: An International Journal, 14, 15–34.

About the Author

Meet Lavonne, a multi-talented artist and certified coach who uses her passion for music and her expertise in trauma recovery to empower women and promote healing. With over 20 years of experience working with vulnerable communities, Lavonne has seen firsthand the impact of trauma on individuals and relationships and is dedicated to providing practical coping tools through an arts-based, healing-centered engagement approach.

Lavonne's journey to becoming an advocate for trauma survivors began with her experiences of using music to cope with trauma. As a singer/songwriter, Lavonne's soulful and powerful vocals convey messages of faith, hope, and healing, creating moments of empowerment and vitality.

Her commitment to helping others find their voice and build resiliency has led her to partner with shelters and reentry programs and share her expertise and voice with organizations in the tri-state area.

Lavonne holds a master of arts degree from Eastern University in organizational leadership and a bachelor's from Rutgers University. She is also a certified women's empowerment & trauma recovery coach and a certified adverse childhood experiences (aces) trainer.

Through her company, Say Something Good LLC, Lavonne continues to provide trauma-informed support to individuals and organizations, bringing change within communities.

For More About Lavonne and Her Speaking, Singing, and Coaching Services, visit:

SaySomethingGoodLLC.com

or Follow Her on Instagram at **@LavonneNichols**

www.ingramcontent.com/pod-product-compliance
Ingram Content Group UK Ltd.
Pitfield, Milton Keynes, MK11 3LW, UK
UKHW020420250726
13967UKWH00007B/2742